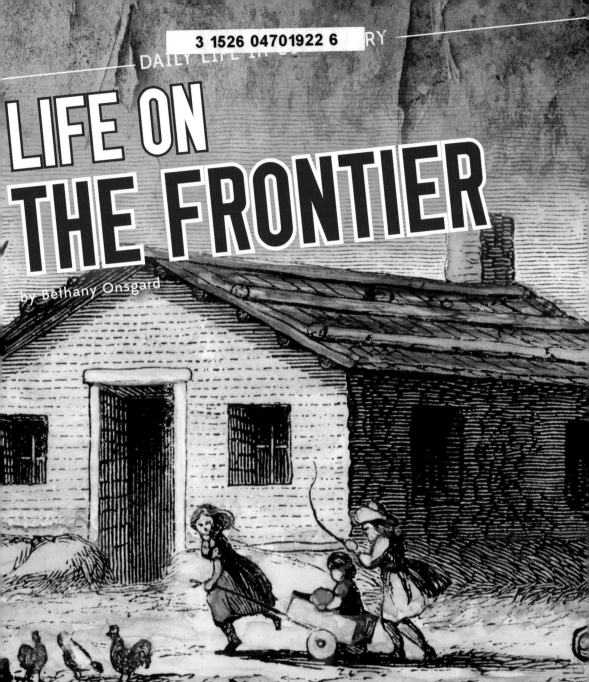

DAILY LIFE IN US HISTORY

LIFE ON
THE FRONTIER

by Bethany Onsgard

Content Consultant
Mark Howard Long
Associate Lecturer, History Department
University of Central Florida

Core Library

An Imprint of Abdo Publishing
www.abdopublishing.com

www.abdopublishing.com

Published by Abdo Publishing, a division of ABDO, PO Box 398166, Minneapolis, Minnesota 55439. Copyright © 2015 by Abdo Consulting Group, Inc. International copyrights reserved in all countries. No part of this book may be reproduced in any form without written permission from the publisher. Core Library™ is a trademark and logo of Abdo Publishing.

Printed in the United States of America, North Mankato, Minnesota
092014
012015

Cover Photo: North Wind Picture Archives/AP Images
Interior Photos: North Wind Picture Archives/AP Images, 1; North Wind Picture Archives, 4, 6, 10, 13, 15, 17, 20, 23, 26, 28, 31, 33, 34, 38, 40, 42, 45; Red Line Editorial, 8; Red Line Editorial/Aaron Amat/Shutterstock Images, 24; Alexander Hay Ritchie/Library of Congress, 36

Editor: Ethan Hiedeman
Series Designer: Becky Daum

Library of Congress Control Number: 2014944206

Cataloging-in-Publication Data
Onsgard, Bethany.
 Life on the frontier / Bethany Onsgard.
  p. cm. -- (Daily life in US history)
 ISBN 978-1-62403-631-6 (lib. bdg.)
 Includes bibliographical references and index.
 1. Frontier and pioneer life--West (U.S.)--Juvenile literature.   2. West (U.S.)--Social conditions--Juvenile literature.   3. West (U.S.)--Social life and customs--Juvenile literature.   I. Title.
 978--dc23
                                              2014944206

CONTENTS

CHAPTER ONE

THE FRONTIER

The covered wagon jostles you awake as it hits a big bump. You ride in the wagon with the food and supplies. You are too young to walk all day like your older brothers and sisters. Your mother rides with you. She cares for your baby sister. The baby is sick. There are no doctors or even towns nearby to go to for help. Your parents told you they were taking a risk by picking up and moving out West onto

The trail to the West was full of hazards, especially for the old, young, and sick.

Pioneers moving west had to deal with dense wilderness and natural obstacles such as the Rocky Mountains.

the frontier. But until your sister got sick you did not understand what they meant.

What Is the Frontier?

This was a common scene for many families that traveled west to make a life on the frontier. The frontier was in the West. It was far away from the big cities in the East such as Boston, Massachusetts, and New York City. The US government defined the frontier as any place that had two or fewer people per square mile. But the so-called frontier was already populated by Native Americans. The Western frontier era lasted roughly from 1803 until 1890, when the US government announced that there was no longer a frontier in the West.

Manifest Destiny

During the 1800s, many Americans believed that all of the land to the west was destined to become part of the United States. Journalist John O. Sullivan first used the term "manifest destiny." He said that it was destined that the United States should add Texas and other territories to the country. Settlers took Sullivan's idea to heart when moving west. They believed that all the land in the West should belong to them, even though hundreds of thousands of Native Americans already lived there. Settlers believed it was their right to force Native Americans out of lands they had lived on for generations.

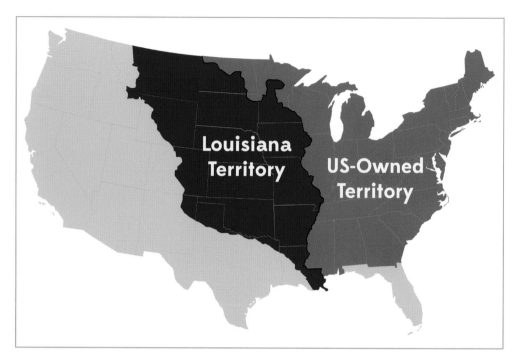

The Louisiana Purchase

This map shows the boundaries of the Louisiana Purchase. How does the map help you better understand the size of the frontier? What do you know about the land contained in the Louisiana Purchase that might have been helpful to scientists and explorers?

The Louisiana Purchase

The American frontier opened up wide with the Louisiana Purchase of 1803. The purchase of land from the French doubled the size of the country. US officials paid $15 million for 828,000 square miles (2,145,000 sq km) of land that stretched from the Mississippi River in the East to the Rocky Mountains in the West.

No one knew everything the land contained. It was a new frontier that Americans were eager to explore. The government sent out nature experts, scientists, and explorers to survey the land and take notes on the animals and people they encountered. Families also moved out to find new opportunities. The government gave people cheap or free land. Families planted, farmed, raised livestock, and built homes on the frontier. An era of westward expansion had begun!

PERSPECTIVES
Lewis and Clark

Meriwether Lewis and William Clark led the first official US expedition through the Louisiana Territory. From May 1804 to September 1806, the group walked, canoed, and forged their way toward the Pacific Ocean. Lewis and Clark took detailed notes about the new plants and animals they encountered. They met and interacted with many groups of Native Americans.

CHAPTER TWO

TRAVELING WEST

The new frontier that Lewis and Clark had explored became home to new settlers. Women, children, and whole families traveled west alongside trappers, fur traders, and explorers. Settlers moved west for new lives and the free land promised by the US government.

Regularly traveled trails were transformed by the constant movement of settlers.

The Homestead Act

One of the main reasons people moved out to the frontier was because of the Homestead Act. The Homestead Act, which was passed in 1862, offered any citizen 160 acres (65 ha) of land in the West for only a small fee. Homesteaders needed to improve the land they bought. This meant they needed to build a house and plant crops on the homestead. If settlers improved their plots of land and stayed there for at least five years, the land became their property. More than 270 million acres (109 million ha) became the property of private citizens under the act.

Trailblazers

Pioneers, or settlers of new land who set out into the frontier, had a long, hard journey in front of them. Wagons carried all of the supplies a family needed. The wagons carried tools, containers for water, spare parts for the wagon, and nearly 1,000 pounds (450 kg) of food. Sometimes settlers packed too much and had to throw things to the side of the road to lighten their load.

The wagons were uncomfortable. The trip was bumpy and the

Everything a family owned was packed onto its wagons and animals for the trip west.

wagons were made entirely of wood. Most settlers walked alongside their wagons. This allowed them to store more weight in the wagons and also to avoid the bumpy ride. Oxen or mules pulled the wagons. These animals could walk farther, could pull more weight, and were less likely to be stolen than horses. Drivers usually walked alongside their oxen to guide them.

Wagon Trains

Often, people traveling west from the same area would set out together in bands or companies. These groups of wagons were called wagon trains. Traveling in a group meant that pioneers had backup in case of danger or hardship. Traveling in a group also meant that settlers had many other people to talk to during the long journey.

The Native Americans that the settlers encountered on their way west were generally friendly. They traded with the settlers, provided needed supplies, and even operated ferries to help settlers get their wagons across rivers. But sometimes, conflicts broke out between Native Americans and settlers. Native Americans usually only attacked wagon trains in retaliation for something the white settlers had done—for example, shooting and killing a Native American. The Native Americans thought their use of violence was justified in these cases.

Hazards of the Trail

Most wagon trains moved slowly, covering only 10 to 12 miles (16–19 km) per day. The journey was very dangerous. The pioneers dealt with delays, including

Harsh weather could bring disaster to unprepared pioneers.

flooded rivers, injured oxen, and sickness. Many people died on the trail west. They were killed by wild animals, drowning, wagon accidents, and sickness.

Disease was a major problem along the trail. There were not many chances to bathe or clean. And safe drinking water was often in short supply. Cholera, a disease spread by water that had been contaminated by animal or human waste, caused many deaths. Poor nutrition also caused many diseases. Some found the trail too hard and turned back east, their dreams of rich new lives crushed by the reality of the harsh conditions.

Settlement Towns

After a long, hard journey, most settlers reached their destinations. Many people went to the Oregon Territory to take advantage of cheap or even free land there. Others went to California, following rumors of gold and good farmland. And many stopped when they found an existing settlement they wanted to be a part of or a piece of land that looked like it could support them.

Those settlers who reached their destinations needed to build homes. At first, most people constructed makeshift houses of stacked logs called half-faced camps. These camps were open in the front and didn't offer protection from the wind or weather. They had three wooden walls and a loose roof or no roof at all. These houses were only temporary. Settlers would live in them while they constructed permanent homes. Most of the land around settlements was

The log cabin came to represent life on the frontier.

heavily wooded, so settlers chopped down trees to build proper log cabins. Often, these had only a few rooms, and the whole family would share one bedroom. Frontier houses had small kitchens, but no bathrooms, running water, or electricity.

Education

Settlements were so small and far apart that most didn't even have schools. Children still needed to learn, though, so many were taught by their parents

Catharine Beecher

One of the most influential educators of this time was Catharine Beecher. In 1852 Beecher started the American Women's Education Association. This association was dedicated to recruiting and training women to teach in frontier schools. Beecher continued to work with the education association until her death in 1878.

at home. Eventually, there were enough children out West to open schoolhouses. Soon, most settlements had one-room schoolhouses, or common schools, where students of all ages gathered and were taught by one teacher. Here, students learned reading, writing, and arithmetic. *Robin Hood, The Swiss Family Robinson*, and *Treasure Island* were all popular books with young readers.

Before the Louisiana Purchase, most teachers were men. As frontier populations grew, there were not enough teachers. Eventually, women began teaching in the common schools. Once schoolhouses were open to females, single women began moving out West to become teachers. But though women were now allowed to teach, female teachers earned less than half the money that male teachers made. There were also laws that made it illegal for married women to teach, so young women had to stop teaching once they got married.

FURTHER EVIDENCE

There is quite a bit of information about traveling west in Chapter Two. What is the main point of this chapter? What key evidence supports this point? Go to the article on pioneers at the website below. Find a quote from the website that supports the chapter's main point. Does the quote support an existing piece of evidence in the chapter? Or does it add a new one? Write a few sentences explaining how the quote you found relates to this chapter.

Wagons West
www.mycorelibrary.com/frontier

CHAPTER THREE

WORK AND SURVIVAL

Even with settlements popping up, most of the frontier was still empty of white settlers. Few people on the frontier had regularly paying jobs. Instead, most frontier settlers made a living off the animals, resources, and land.

Fur Trapping

Lewis and Clark encountered many animals on their travels. As people learned about these animals, they

Many made their fortunes on the frontier trapping animals and selling their pelts.

saw that money could be made from them. Hundreds of men set off into the wilderness to trap animals—mostly beavers—for their pelts, or skins and furs. The fur trade became one of the biggest moneymakers on the American frontier.

Fur trappers gathered furs that would be made into clothes for the rich. But fur trappers, often called mountain men, lived rough, isolated lives. Most mountain men traveled alone, but a few moved together in small groups. They spent

Mountain men lived harsh lives in the wilderness.

months, even years out in the wilderness. They ate whatever food they hunted or found, including deer, fish, and mountain goats.

Native Americans Lose the Bison

Native Americans had been living off the land that settlers were just discovering for thousands of years. Bison meat and fur had long sustained Native

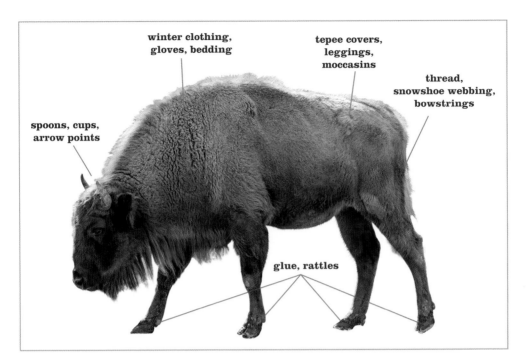

winter clothing, gloves, bedding

tepee covers, leggings, moccasins

thread, snowshoe webbing, bowstrings

spoons, cups, arrow points

glue, rattles

Bison

Native Americans used nearly every part of any animal that they hunted. Does seeing the different things Native Americans made from bison give you a greater appreciation for how important the animals were to them? How do you think Native Americans' lives were changed when they could no longer hunt bison?

Americans who lived on the Great Plains. Almost every part of the bison was useful for daily life.

Eventually white settlers hunted bison nearly to extinction. By 1889, approximately 1,000 bison remained alive in all of North America. The Native

Americans could no longer rely on giant bison herds for survival.

Ranches

All of the open, grassy space on the frontier was perfect for raising cattle. Settlers bought large areas of land from the government to use as ranches, or places to raise livestock. Ranchers would have hundreds or even thousands of cows. They hired ranch hands to help tend the animals. Often these ranch hands were single men who lived and worked together at the ranch. The men shared small bunkhouses that were frigidly cold in the winter and sweltering hot in the summer.

The Oregon Trail

The Oregon Trail was a path that hundreds of thousands of settlers followed from Independence, Missouri, to new settlements in Oregon from the 1840s to the 1860s. The 2,000-mile (3,200-km) trail provided an established route that settlers could follow without needing to hire a guide. The trail followed the Platte, Snake, and Columbia rivers so settlers could use them as sources of water. Settlers on the trail grazed livestock on the prairie grass, hunted bison and antelope, and fished the rivers for sustenance.

Cowboys were in charge of keeping watch over many cattle at once.

These ranch hands were known as cowboys. In the early 1800s, most cowboys were white men from the East Coast. After the end of the Civil War (1861–1865), freed African-American slaves began to move west, looking for opportunities. Some of these men became cowboys. By 1865, nearly one-fourth of the cowboys on the frontier were African Americans.

Cowboys rode horses and kept watch over the herd, keeping them safe from other settlers and predatory animals. Cowboys woke up at sunrise and spent long, 18-hour days in the saddle.

If you took a road trip today, you would have many things to entertain you. Without iPods, or even radios, the first Americans to travel out into the frontier had to keep themselves entertained. One of the most popular ways to pass the time was to sing. Below are a few stanzas from the famous frontier song "The Cowboy":

All day long on the prairies I ride,
Not even a dog to trot by my side;
My fire I kindle with chips gathered round,
My coffee I boil without being ground.

I wash in a pool and wipe on a sack;
I carry my wardrobe all on my back;
For want of an oven I cook bread in a pot,
And sleep on the ground for want of a cot.

Source: "Cowboy Songs & Frontier Ballads." Legends of America. *Legends of America,* 2014. Web. Accessed August 11, 2014.

What's the Big Idea?

Take a close look at the lyrics to "The Cowboy." What is the singer's main point about life as a cowboy? Pick out two details that back up this point. What does the song tell you about what life was like for a cowboy?

CHAPTER FOUR

FRONTIER FOOD AND FUN

Life was hard on the frontier, but it wasn't all work. Settlers went shopping, bought supplies, and socialized with friends. They just did these things a little bit differently than people do today.

Food

There were no grocery stores out on the frontier. Any food that a settler wanted to put on the table had to be grown, foraged, or hunted. Settlers planted

Pioneers often cooked their meals over outdoor fires.

Laura Ingalls Wilder

Many people know about life on the frontier because of Laura Ingalls Wilder. Wilder was born in Wisconsin in 1867. She lived with her family in Kansas, Minnesota, and later Iowa. Wilder grew up to be a writer, and she turned her family's stories into a popular series of books. Each one of her books focuses on one of the places her family lived. She began with *Little House in the Big Woods*, about her life in Pepin, Wisconsin. Wilder showed readers what it was like to grow up on the frontier. The books became so popular that they were turned into a television show, *Little House on the Prairie*, in 1974.

backyard gardens, which they called kitchen gardens. Kitchen gardens provided almost all of the food they ate. Most pioneers planted two gardens—one in the spring and one in the summer. The spring garden gave homesteaders leafy greens, peas, and light foods like radishes. The summer garden had a heartier yield. It gave gardeners squash, beets, and root vegetables that would keep throughout a long winter. Settlers had to be careful with

Native Americans traded pelts and other valuables at trading posts.

their food and ration it throughout the year. Settlers canned or pickled anything that wasn't eaten right away to eat later.

Shopping

Shopping trips on the frontier were nothing like running errands today. Settlements didn't have grocery stores, malls, or markets. Instead settlers would travel to the nearest trading post, which was usually many miles away. The trip to town might take settlers days, so many went only once or twice a year to stock up on supplies. The trading post had all of the things that a family could not make for itself, such as coffee, flour, and fabric. If a family ran out of something, they had to do without until the next trip.

Serials

Serials were book-length stories published in small chunks in magazines. Families looked forward to the next piece of their favorite serial. These were delivered in the mail and so could take a long time to get to the frontier. It wasn't easy getting mail all the way across the country. Sometimes weeks would go by without any mail making it to the frontier. Families were left waiting to see what would happen to their favorite characters. Henry James and Herman Melville are among the American writers who published serials in magazines.

Entertainment

With no TV, no computers, and no town to go out in and explore, settlers needed to find ways to entertain themselves. One of the most popular activities on the frontier was reading. People subscribed to magazines

Sewing circles and other activities were opportunities for socialization.

and serial novels. Settlers looked forward to the delivery every month. Reading was an activity for the whole family, and parents often read out loud to their children.

Frontier settlers were skilled at turning any chore or activity into an excuse to socialize. If there was a lot of corn to husk or a huge field of crops to be harvested, settlers invited all of the pioneers in the area over. They would divide up the work, making it go faster. This also gave people a chance to talk, gossip, and have fun with their fellow settlers.

CHAPTER FIVE

NATIVE AMERICANS ON THE FRONTIER

Eventually the frontier became an established part of the United States. US settlers moved into the Great Plains. They built small towns and big cities. White Americans were finding great success on the frontier, but there were often consequences for other groups living in the area, especially Native American tribes.

Native Americans and white settlers often had tumultuous relationships.

Andrew Jackson removed Native Americans from their territory over the objections of the US Supreme Court.

Culture Clash

While white Americans settled the frontier, they drove Native Americans out. Settlers forced Native American peoples farther and farther west. Americans believed they had a right to any land they could claim. At this time, Native Americans were not counted as citizens of the United States. The government signed treaties with Native Americans, promising them land farther west if they left the Eastern lands they had been living on for thousands of years. Most treaties deceived and manipulated the Native Americans. The Native Americans often did not understand what they were signing. They had a different understanding of land ownership. They did not understand what it meant to sell their land away. Some treaties simply shrank Native American lands, leaving them with a fraction of their former lands. Policies toward Native American lands shifted greatly over time.

In 1830 President Andrew Jackson signed

The Trail of Tears

When Native American tribes wouldn't leave their land, the government pushed them out. In 1839 Cherokee Indians living in the Southeast, especially Georgia, were rounded up by US soldiers and forced to walk west. They walked as far as 1,500 miles (2,400 km). The trip was hard, and the soldiers were violent with the Native Americans, even the women and children. Thousands of Native Americans died while making the journey to Indian Territory. Today this route is called the Trail of Tears because of its devastating effect on the Cherokee population.

Many Native Americans were forced to move long distances off their land.

the Indian Removal Act. This gave the government the power to forcibly remove any Native Americans from their land without negotiating with Native American leaders.

Reservations

Many Native Americans were forced to live on reservations. Within these protected areas, Native Americans were free to govern themselves and make their own decisions, but they were not allowed to leave the assigned areas. The lands were often of poor quality and unwanted by white settlers. Today there are more than 300 Native American reservations in the United States. Native Americans now largely govern themselves on their reservations. Most of these reservations are west of the Mississippi River, where American Indians were forced to move as settlers pushed them out of the East.

PERSPECTIVES

The Second Seminole War

In 1835, war broke out between the Seminole Native Americans and the United States when most Seminoles refused to leave their lands in Florida and move west of the Mississippi River. The Seminoles hid in the Everglades, a large swamp and grassland 50 miles (80 km) wide covering much of southern Florida. They carried out small and quick attacks on larger US forces. Seminoles killed approximately 2,000 US soldiers in the fighting. The Seminoles only gave up and agreed to move when their leader, Osceola, was captured in 1837. But some Seminoles stayed behind and continued to live and fight in Florida.

Many of the pioneers' log cabins eventually gave way to towns and cities.

The Closing of the Frontier

In 1890 a US Census official said that there were so many settlements in the western United States that there was no longer a frontier line. The United States' last great growth spurt had left it bigger, wealthier, and with a frontier spirit that would define the nation for decades to come.

Private John G. Burnett was a white soldier who had many Cherokee friends. But as a soldier, he was ordered to help force the Native Americans out of their lands. Below is an excerpt from Burnett's journal from December 11, 1890:

> On the morning of November the 17th we encountered a terrific sleet and snow storm with freezing temperatures and from that day until we reached the end of the fateful journey on March the 26th, 1839, the sufferings of the Cherokees were awful. The trail of the exiles was a trail of death. They had to sleep in the wagons and on the ground without fire. And I have known as many as twenty-two of them to die in one night of pneumonia due to ill treatment, cold, and exposure.

Source: Burnett, John G. "A soldier recalls the Trail of Tears." Learn NC. UNC School of Education. Web. Accessed August 11, 2014.

Changing Minds

This text passage discusses treatment of Native Americans on the Trail of Tears. Take a position on whether Native Americans should have been forced to leave their land. Then imagine that your best friend has the opposite opinion. Write a short essay trying to change your friend's mind. Make sure you detail your opinion and your reasons for it. Include facts and details that support your reasons.

A DAY IN THE LIFE

William is a cowboy in Texas in 1870 who works driving cattle to a trading post to be sold at market. Each day is long and hard. William spends most of his time alone with the cattle.

4:00 a.m.
William wakes up after a night of sleeping under the stars. With only a small pack to use as a pillow, sleeping out on the frontier is not comfortable for a cowboy. William is still a bit tired when he wakes.

4:30 a.m.
William eats a quick breakfast of bread and dried meat. Cowboys are out riding for days, even weeks at a time, and need to pack food that won't spoil.

5:00 a.m.
Time to herd the cattle! While William was sleeping, another cowboy watched the cows to make sure they didn't wander off.

7:00 a.m.
William and the other cowboys lead the cattle over hills, through the prairie, and along winding streams. Cowboys get to see a lot of beautiful wilderness.

12:30 p.m.
After hours on a horse, William finally gets a break. The cowboys stop for a quick lunch and let the horses rest.

1:00 p.m.
Back on the trail! There are other cowboys watching the herd with William, but they are very spread out, guarding the cattle from all sides. William rides at the back of the herd, making sure that none of the cows fall behind. He rides in silence for hours.

7:00 p.m.
A coyote darts out from the woods, spooking the herd of cattle. The cowboys need to round up the cows before any run away. The cowboys ride the horses in a circle around the cattle, keeping them in one place.

9:00 p.m.
As it gets dark, the cowboys find a safe place to stop and rest for the evening. William is tired after a long day of riding, but someone needs to stay up and guard the livestock. While the rest of the cowboys go to sleep, William stays up to keep watch.

Why Do I Care?

Americans moved onto the frontier more than 200 years ago. But you can still learn a lot from their journeys and experiences. How does the settlement of the frontier affect your life today? Are there cities or professions that might not exist without that period? How might your life be different if the Louisiana Purchase had never happened? Use your imagination!

Take a Stand

Chapter Five discusses the treatment of Native Americans during the 1800s. Do you think the US government had the right to force Native Americans to leave the land they had lived on for thousands of years? Or should American settlers have tried to live alongside the Native Americans? Write a short essay explaining your opinion. Make sure to give reasons for your opinion, and facts and details to support those reasons.

You Are There

This book shares details about life in a settlement town. Imagine that you are a boy or a girl who just moved to a frontier settlement with your family. You don't yet have a house, and there are no stores to shop in. How do you feel about your new surroundings? What do you do for fun?

Say What?

Studying different time periods can mean learning a lot of new vocabulary. Find five words in this book that you've never heard before. Use a dictionary to find out what they mean. Then write the meanings in your own words, and use each word in a new sentence.

GLOSSARY

frontier line
a line marking where "frontier" ends and "territory" begins

pioneers
settlers who traveled west to make new lives on the frontier

settlements
new towns or villages where people move to start new lives

homestead
a piece of land acquired from US public lands by living on and cultivating it

survey
to study and explore a piece of land

pelts
usually unfinished skins with its hair, wool, or fur still attached

trading post
a station or store of a trader or trading company established in a thinly settled region where local products (such as furs) are exchanged for manufactured goods

LEARN MORE

Books

Domnauer, Teresa. *Life in the West*. New York: Scholastic, 2010.

Schlissel, Lillian. *Black Frontiers: A History of African American Heroes in the Old West*. New York: Aladdin, 2000.

Yasuda, Anita. *Westward Expansion of the United States: 1801–1861*. Mankato, MN: ABDO, 2014.

Websites

To learn more about Daily Life in US History, visit **booklinks.abdopublishing.com**. These links are routinely monitored and updated to provide the most current information available.

Visit **www.mycorelibrary.com** for free additional tools for teachers and students.

INDEX

ABOUT THE AUTHOR

Bethany Onsgard works in publishing and spends her days reading, writing, and exploring the outdoors in beautiful Portland, Oregon.